SUPERSTARS of WRESTLING

THE MIZ

BY BENJAMIN PROUDFIT

Gareth Stevens
PUBLISHING

HOT TOPICS

Please visit our website, www.garethstevens.com. For a free color catalog of all our high-quality books, call toll free 1-800-542-2595 or fax 1-877-542-2596.

Cataloging-in-Publication Data

Names: Proudfit, Benjamin.
Title: The Miz / Benjamin Proudfit.
Description: New York : Gareth Stevens Publishing, 2019. | Series: Superstars of wrestling | Includes glossary and index.
Identifiers: LCCN ISBN 9781538221136 (pbk.) | ISBN 9781538221112 (library bound) | ISBN 9781538221143 (6 pack)
Subjects: LCSH: Miz, 1980---Juvenile literature. | Wrestlers--United States--Biography--Juvenile literature.
Classification: LCC GV1196.M59 P67 2019 | DDC 796.812092 B--dc23

First Edition

Published in 2019 by
Gareth Stevens Publishing
111 East 14th Street, Suite 349
New York, NY 10003

Copyright © 2019 Gareth Stevens Publishing

Designer: Sarah Liddell
Editor: Kristen Nelson

Photo credits: Cover, p. 1 George Napolitano/Contributor/FilmMagic/Getty Images; p. 5 Moses Robinson/Contributor/Getty Images Entertainment/Getty Images; pp. 7, 21 Joern Pollex/Staff/Bongarts/Getty Images; p. 9 Barry King/Contributor/WireImage/ Getty Images; p. 11 Ron Galella/Contributor/Ron Galella Collection/Getty Images; p. 13 Gabe Palacio/Staff/Getty Images Entertainment/Getty Images; p. 15 Chris Ryan - Corbis/Contributor/Corbis Sport/Getty Images; p. 17 Ethan Miller/Staff/ Getty Images Entertainment/Getty Images; p. 19 Maurilbert/Wikimedia Commons; p. 23 Flickr upload bot/Wikimedia Commons; p. 25 Edge4life42/Wikimedia Commons; p. 27 THOMAS SAMSON/Stringer/AFP/Getty Images; p. 29 Prof. Professorson/ Wikimedia Commons.

Printed in the United States of America

CPSIA compliance information: Batch #CS18GS: For further information contact Gareth Stevens, New York, New York at 1-800-542-2595.

CONTENTS

AWESOME!

AWESOME!

The Miz is the biggest talker in World Wrestling Entertainment (WWE). He's always telling everyone how awesome he is! But behind the scenes, The Miz has worked hard to prove himself in the ring, both to his fans and to other wrestlers.

IN THE RING

"Every ounce of respect I have today,
I had to earn," The Miz said in 2017.

5

GROWING UP

The Miz was born Michael Mizanin on October 8, 1980. He lived in the city of Parma outside of Cleveland, Ohio. His dad owned several Mr. Hero sandwich shops. The Miz always thought when he grew up, he might take over the family business.

IN THE RING

As a kid, The Miz was a big fan
of **professional** wrestling.

7

While in high school, The Miz played a lot of sports. He was even captain of the basketball and cross-country teams. After high school, The Miz went to college at the Miami University of Ohio.

IN THE RING

In college, The Miz studied business.

8

9

While in college, The Miz found out that MTV was **casting** the next season of their show *The Real World*. He sent in a video—and was chosen! The Miz appeared on the 10th season, *Back to New York*, in 2001.

IN THE RING

In 2001, there were far fewer **reality** TV
shows than there are today. At that time, people on
The Real World were often very well known!

THE MIZ IS

THE MIZ IS BORN

The Miz had trouble getting along with his castmates in the *Real World* house. So, he started pretending to be a big-time pro wrestler called The Miz. That was the beginning of his path to becoming a WWE Superstar!

IN THE RING

The Miz was popular on MTV. He was
part of *Fear Factor* as well as many seasons of
The Real World/Road Rules Challenge.

13

WRESTLING SCHOOL

In 2003, The Miz started
training to be a wrestler.
He went to Ultimate Pro
Wrestling, which was in
Southern California. At first,
The Miz wasn't the best. But
he worked hard and soon
began to get noticed.

JOHN
CENA

IN THE RING

The Miz wasn't the only future WWE Superstar at Ultimate Pro Wrestling. John Cena was training there, too!

15

TOUGH ENOUGH

In 2004, WWE called The Miz to be part of the 4th season of their **competition** reality show *Tough Enough*. He did well in front of the cameras as well as in the ring. The Miz came in second on his season.

IN THE RING

The Miz showed enough **talent** on *Tough Enough* to be offered a contract from WWE. He started working for WWE's Deep South Wrestling in Georgia.

17

TAG TEAM CHAMPS

The Miz started on WWE's main **roster** in 2006. He won a match on *SmackDown* against Tatanka! In 2007, The Miz started working in a tag team with John Morrison. They won the WWE Tag Team Championship!

JOHN MORRISON

IN THE RING

The Miz has often been a host in WWE, too. He hosted the Diva Search, which looked for new WWE Divas, or female wrestlers. He met his wife, Maryse, there!

19

GOING SOLO

The Miz and John Morrison lost their titles in 2008. But, they won the World Tag Team Championship not long after. By 2009, The Miz was ready for a singles championship. On *Raw*, he beat Kofi Kingston for the US title!

IN THE RING

The Miz was already well known when he came to WWE. Some other wrestlers didn't like that. The Miz has said he had to work twice as hard to show that he should be part of WWE.

21

MR. MONEY IN THE BANK

The Miz won the Money in the Bank contract in a ladder match in July 2010. He cashed it in a few months later and won his first WWE Championship! In April 2011, he **defended** his title in the main event of WrestleMania 27!

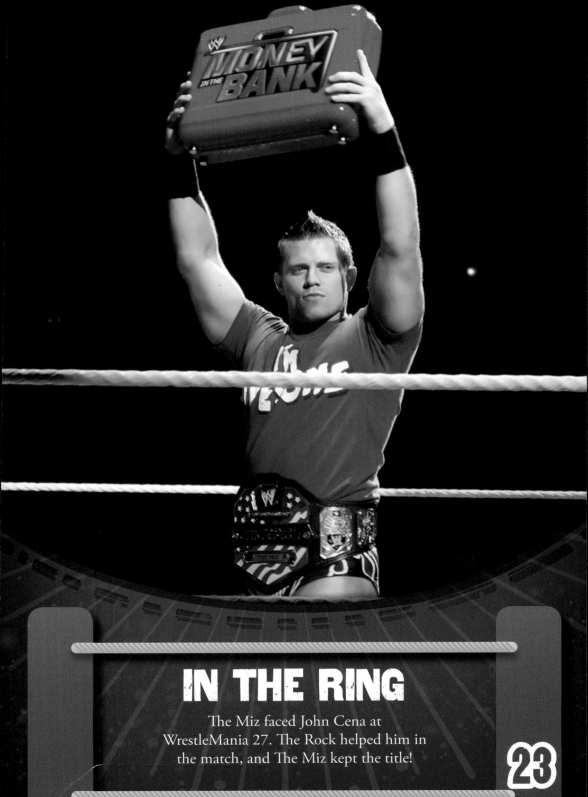

IN THE RING

The Miz faced John Cena at
WrestleMania 27. The Rock helped him in
the match, and The Miz kept the title!

23

INTERCONTINENTAL REIGN

The Miz lost the WWE Championship to John Cena at the Extreme Rules **pay-per-view** soon after WrestleMania 27. But in July 2012, he won his first Intercontinental Championship on *Raw*. This gave him a "grand slam" of titles in WWE!

IN THE RING

The Miz has starred in movies made by WWE
including *The Marine 3: Homefront, Christmas Bounty,
The Marine 4: Moving Target,* and *Santa's Little Helper.*

25

The Miz won the Intercontinental Championship several more times! In 2016, Superstar Zac Ryder beat him for the title in a seven-man ladder match at WrestleMania 32. But the next day, The Miz defeated Zac Ryder and won it!

MARYSE

IN THE RING

The Miz and Maryse were married in 2014. The
day after WrestleMania 32, Maryse began working
as her husband's manager on TV. She helped
him win the title from Zac Ryder!

27

DREAMS COME TRUE

The Miz worked hard to go from wrestling fan to WWE Superstar. His story is a great example for those looking to accomplish big dreams. The Miz has said: "It just goes to show that with hard work, **sacrifice**, dreams do come true."

IN THE RING

The Miz and Maryse wrestled as a tag team at WrestleMania 33 in 2017. They lost to Nikki Bella and John Cena, but they had the chance to compete in the biggest pay-per-view of the year together!

29

THE BEST OF THE MIZ

SIGNATURE MOVES
clothesline, snap DDT, reality check

FINISHERS
skull-crushing finale, figure-four leglock

ACCOMPLISHMENTS
WWE World Champion, Intercontinental Champion, US Champion, Tag Team Champion, Money in the Bank winner

MATCH TO WATCH
Wrestlemania 27 vs. John Cena

FOR MORE INFORMATION

BOOKS

Doeden, Matt. *The Miz: Pro Wrestling Superstar*. North Mankato, MN: Capstone Press, 2014.

Markegard, Blake. *The Miz*. Minneapolis, MN: Bellwether Media, Inc., 2015.

WEBSITES

The Miz
www.wwe.com/superstars/the-miz
Keep track of The Miz on his official WWE webpage.

WWE Profile: The Miz
www.espn.com/wwe/story/_/id/17167441/wwe-profile-page-miz
Read the latest news about The Miz in WWE on his ESPN profile.

GLOSSARY

cast: to choose for a TV show or movie

competition: an event in which people try to win

defend: to keep from losing something

pay-per-view: an event that can only be seen on a TV channel if viewers pay a fee

professional: earning money from an activity that many people do for fun

reality: having to do with real events or situations

roster: the list of people that are on a team

sacrifice: a giving up of something, which allows someone else to receive something

talent: skillfulness

INDEX